HAL•LEONARD

Pro Vocal®
BETTER THAN KARAOKE!

WOMEN'S EDITION - VOLUME 14

Musicals of BOUBLIL & SCHÖNBERG

T0066115

Dramatic Performance Rights controlled and licensed by
Cameron Mackintosh (Overseas) Ltd.
One Bedford Square, London WC1B 3RA England
Tel 44 (0) 20 7637 8866 Fax 44 (0) 20 7436 2683

Stock and Amateur Performance Rights are licensed by
Music Theater International, Inc.
545 Eighth Avenue, New York, New York 10018
Tel (212) 868-6668 Fax (212) 643-8465

Non-Dramatic and Concert Performance
Rights are controlled by
Alain Boublil Music Ltd. and licensed by the American Society
of Composers, Authors and Publishers (ASCAP),
One Lincoln Plaza, New York, New York 10023
Tel (212) 595-3050 Fax (212)787-1381

ISBN-13: 978-1-4234-1642-5
ISBN-10: 1-4234-1642-2

HAL•LEONARD®
CORPORATION
7777 W. BLUEMOUND RD. P.O. BOX 13819 MILWAUKEE, WI 53213

Visit Hal Leonard Online at
www.halleonard.com

Castle on a Cloud

from LES MISÉRABLES

Music by Claude-Michel Schönberg

Lyrics by Alain Boublil, Jean-Marc Natel and Herbert Kretzmer

I Dreamed a Dream

from LES MISÉRABLES
Music by Claude-Michel Schönberg
Lyrics by Alain Boublil, Jean-Marc Natel and Herbert Kretzmer

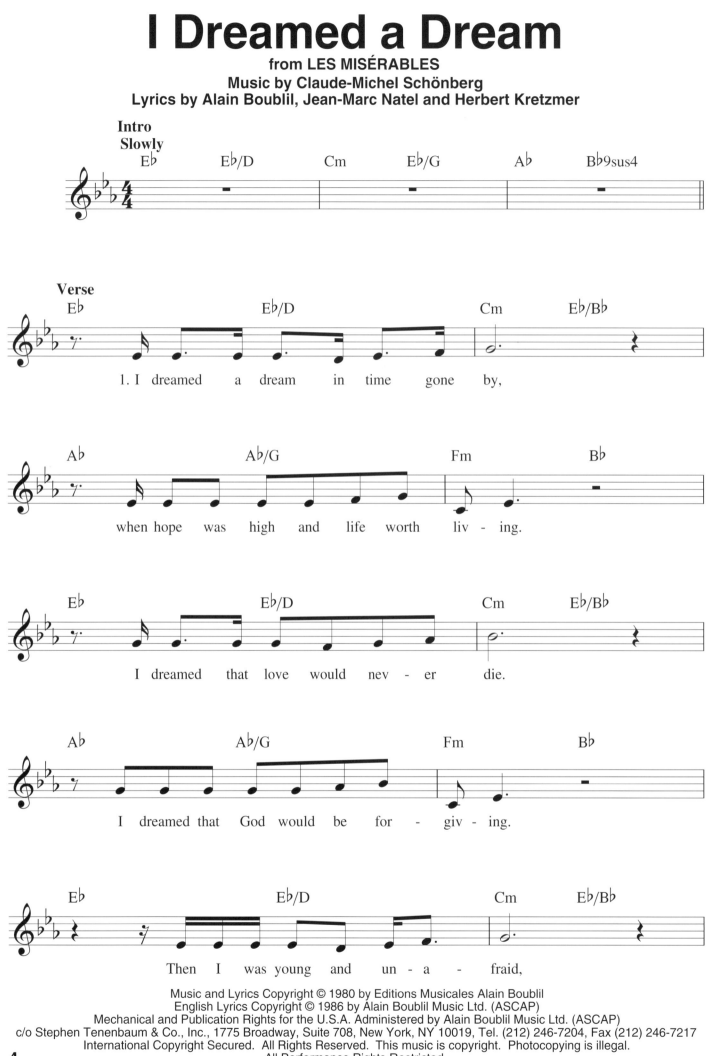

Outro-Verse

I'd Give My Life for You

from MISS SAIGON

Music by Claude-Michel Schönberg
Lyrics by Richard Maltby Jr. and Alain Boublil
Adapted from original French Lyrics by Alain Boublil

To make sure you're not hurt a - gain. _____

I swear I'll give my life for you. _____

I've tast - ed love be - yond all fear.

And you should know it's love that brought you ___ here. And in one per - fect

night when the stars burned like new, I knew what I must do. ___ I'll

A tempo

give you _____ a mil - lion things I'll nev - er own, I'll

give you a world to con - quer ___ when you're grown.

You will be who you want to be. _____ You

In My Life

from LES MISÉRABLES
Music by Claude-Michel Schönberg
Lyrics by Herbert Kretzmer
Original Text by Alain Boublil and Jean-Marc Natel

The Last Night of the World

from MISS SAIGON

Music by Claude-Michel Schönberg
Lyrics by Richard Maltby Jr. and Alain Boublil
Adapted from original French Lyrics by Alain Boublil

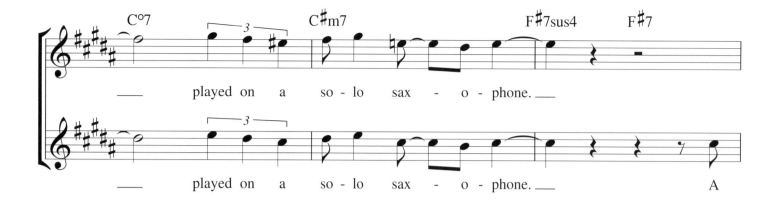

played on a so-lo sax - o - phone. ___

played on a so-lo sax - o - phone. ___ A

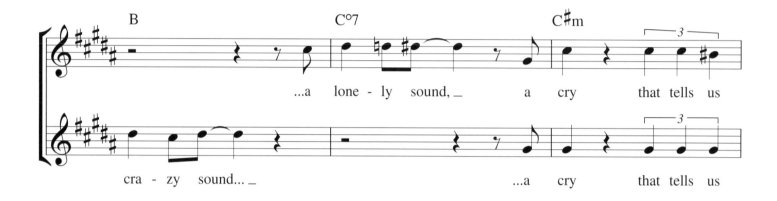

...a lone-ly sound, ___ a cry that tells us

cra - zy sound... ___ ...a cry that tells us

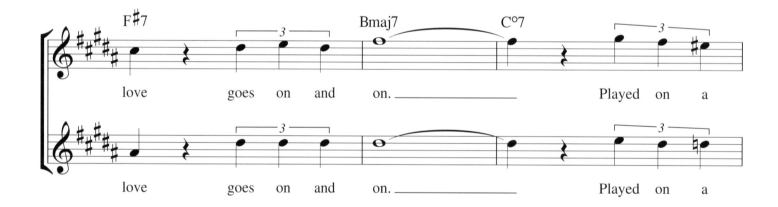

love goes on and on. _____ Played on a

love goes on and on. _____ Played on a

so - lo sax - o - phone, ___ it's tell-ing me ___ to

so - lo sax - o - phone, ___ it's tell-ing me ___ to

ev - er knew. ___

Dreams _____ you won't need _____ when I'm through.

An - y - where we may be, I will sing ___ with you ___

An - y - where we may be, I will sing ___ with you ___

Outro-Chorus

___ our _____ song. _____

___ our _____ song. _____

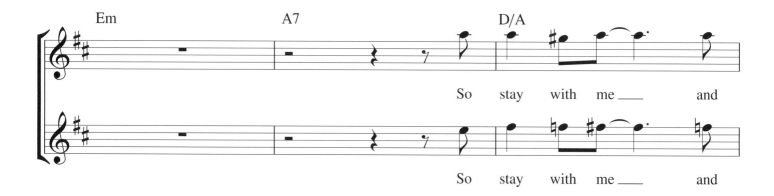

So stay with me ___ and

So stay with me ___ and

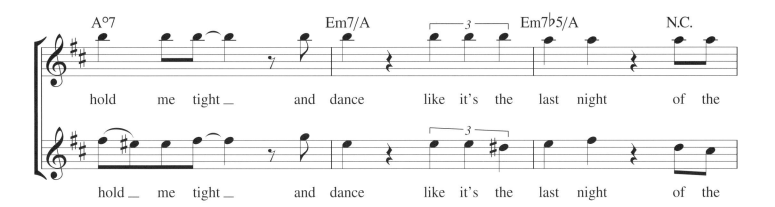

hold me tight __ and dance like it's the last night of the

hold __ me tight __ and dance like it's the last night of the

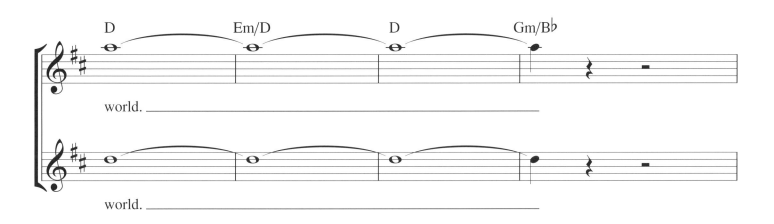

world. _____

world. _____

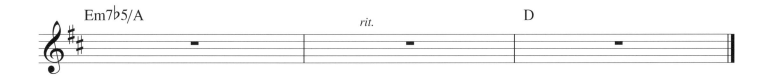

Now That I've Seen Her

from MISS SAIGON
Music by Claude-Michel Schönberg
Lyrics by Richard Maltby Jr. and Alain Boublil
Adapted from original French Lyrics by Alain Boublil

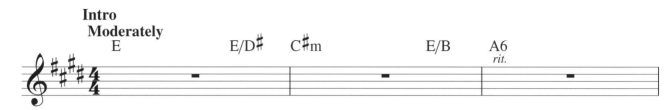

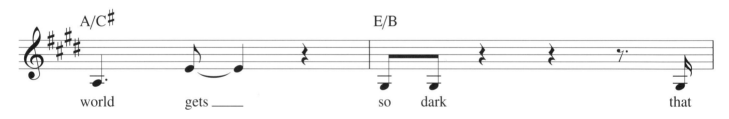

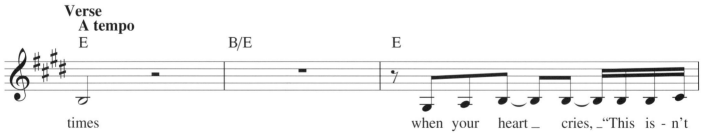

C#m   E/B   A   F#m   B7   *rit.*

___,   In   her

Bridge
A tempo

E   B/E   E7

eyes,   in   her   voice,

A/C#   F#m7   G#7

in   the   heat _____ that   filled   the   air,   part   of

C#m   F#m7b5/C

him _____ still   lin - gers   there.

E/B   *3*   B

I   know   what   pain   her   life   to - day   must   be,

Bm   D/E   E   A

but   if   it   all   comes   down   to   her   or   me,   I   won't

Am   Am6   E/B   B

wait,   I   swear   I'll

fight. _____

Chorus

Now that ___ I've seen her, ___ she's more than ___ a

name. She is not some fling from long a - go. ___

Now that ___ I've seen her, ___ I can't stay ___ the

same. Who's the man that I al - ways trust - ed?

Now I have to know. _____

On My Own

from LES MISÉRABLES

Music by Claude-Michel Schönberg
Lyrics by Alain Boublil, John Caird, Trevor Nunn,
Jean-Marc Natel and Herbert Kretzmer

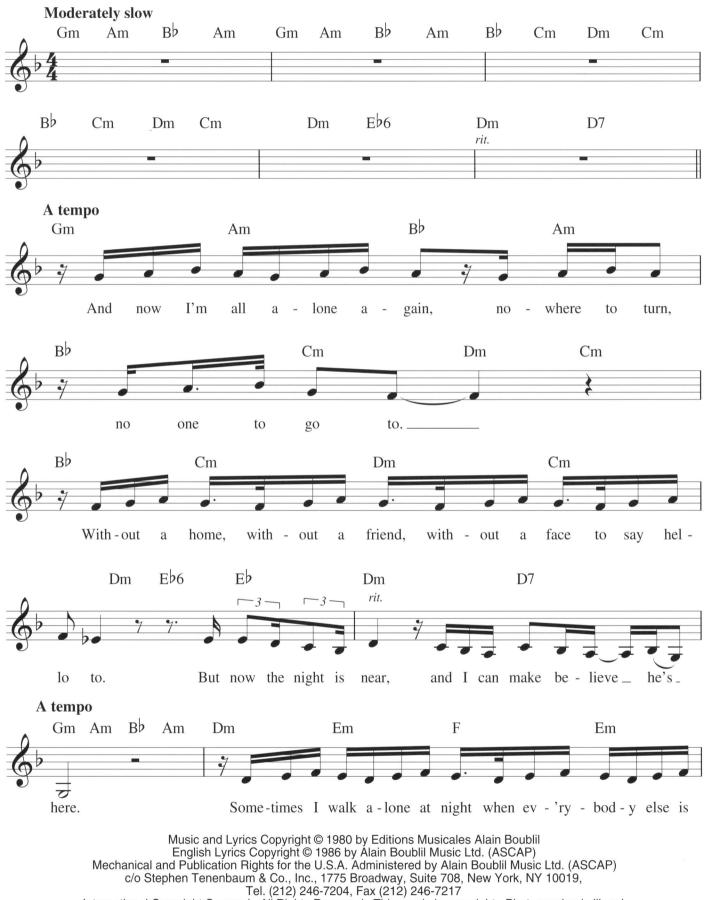

out him ___ the world a - round me chang - es. ___ The
trees are bare and ev - 'ry - where the streets are full of
strang - ers. ___ I love him ___ but ev - 'ry - day ___ I'm ___
___ learn - ing, ___ all my life I've on - ly been pre -
tend - ing. _____ With - out me ___ his world will go on

Freely

turn - ing, ___ the world is full of hap - pi - ness that I have nev - er
known. I love him, I love him, I
love _ him, ___ but on - ly on my _ own.

How Many Tears?

from MARTIN GUERRE

Music by Claude-Michel Schönberg
Lyrics by Alain Boublil and Stephen Clark

tears through the years can I cry?

How man - y tears un - til my heart runs

dry? Through the fights that a wom - an must

fight, on - ly to do what she

feels must be right. Some - times I

won - der if some - one hears.

Why must I live through so man - y

A tempo

tears? _____

Sabbath, Bloody Sabbath

Words and Music by Frank Iommi, John Osbourne, William Ward and Terence Butler

Tune down 1 1/2 steps:
(low to high) C#-F#-B-E-G#-C#

Intro
Moderately slow Rock ♩ = 66

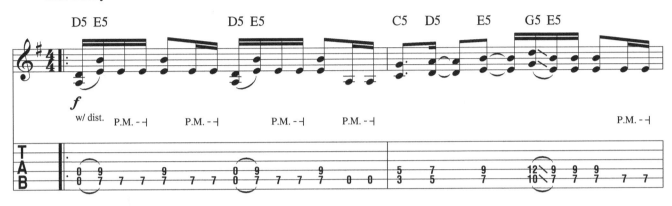

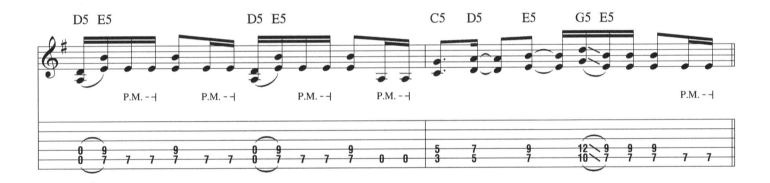

Verse

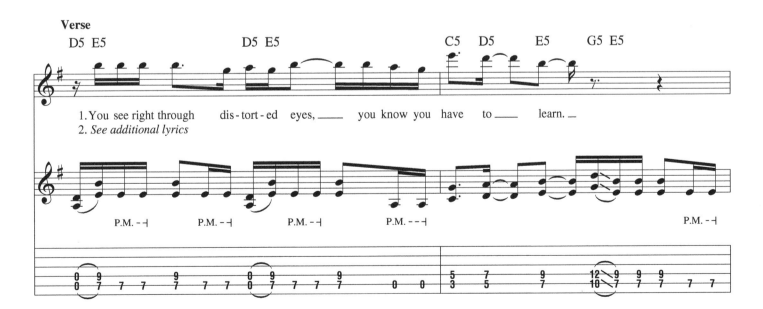

1. You see right through dis-tort-ed eyes, ___ you know you have to ___ learn. ___
2. *See additional lyrics*

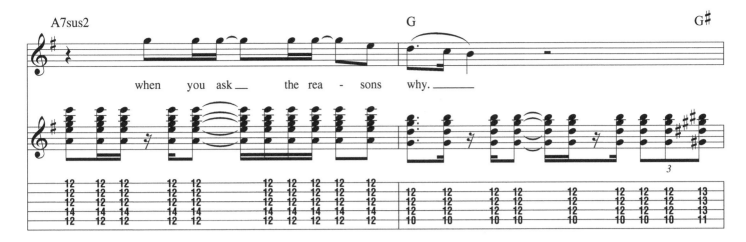

when you ask___ the rea - sons why.___

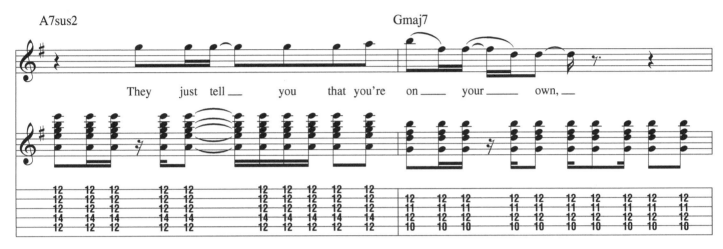

They just tell___ you that you're on___ your___ own,___

fill your head___ all___ full of___ lies.___

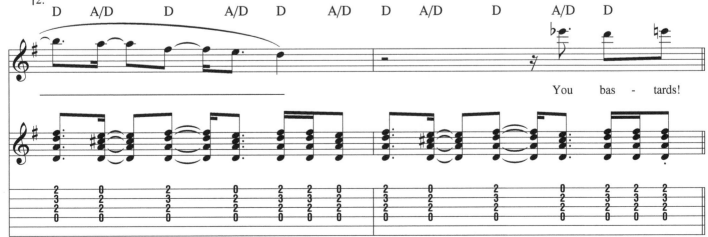

You bas - tards!

Guitar Solo

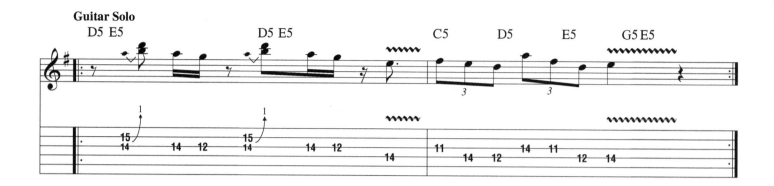

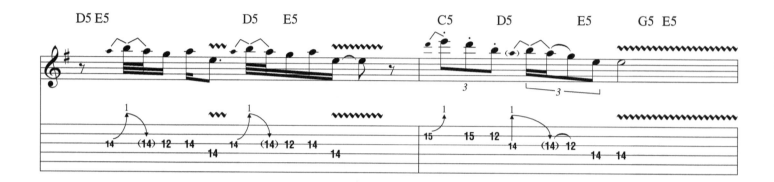

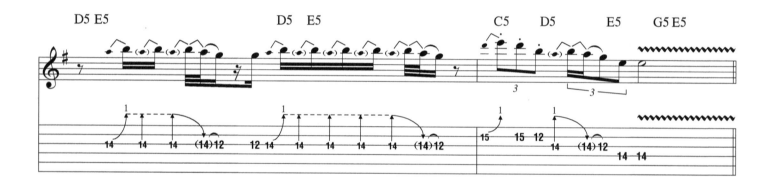

Interlude

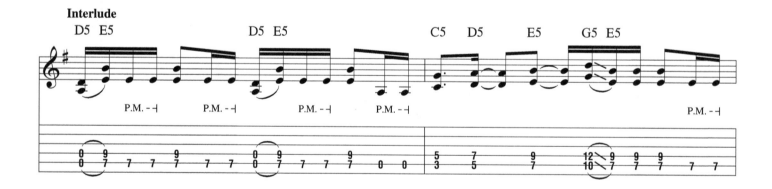

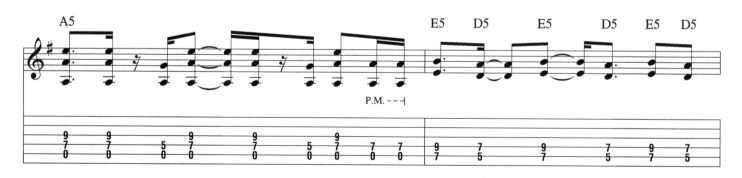

10

Bridge

Where __
See additional lyrics

__   can   you   run __   to?   What   more   can you   do? __

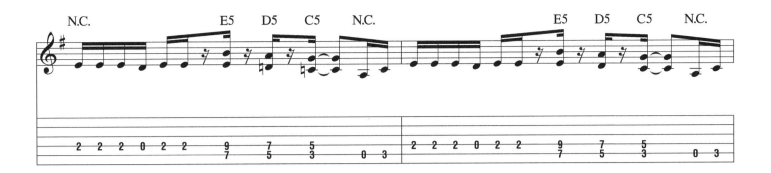

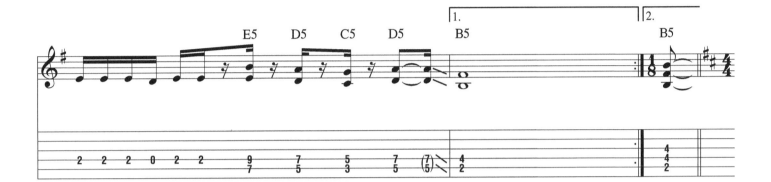

Repeat and fade

Outro
Double-time feel

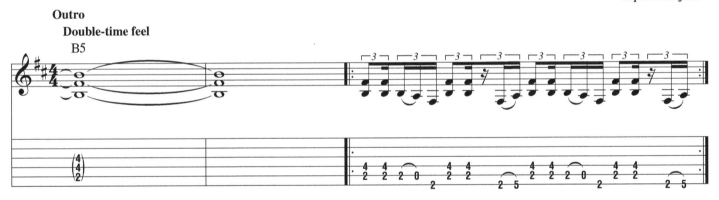

Additional Lyrics

2. The people who have crippled you,
   You wanna see them burn.
   The gates of life have closed on you
   And there's just no return.
   You're wishing that the hands of doom
   Could take your mind away,
   And you don't care if you don't see
   Again the light of day.

Bridge Ev'rything around you, what's it coming to?
   God knows as your dog knows,
   Bog blast all of you.
   Sabbath, bloody Sabbath,
   Nothing more to do.
   Living just for dying,
   Dying just for you, yeah.

Children of the Grave

Words and Music by Frank Iommi, William Ward, John Osbourne and Terence Butler

Tune down 1 1/2 steps:
(low to high) C# F# B E G# C#

Intro
Moderate Rock ♩ = 146

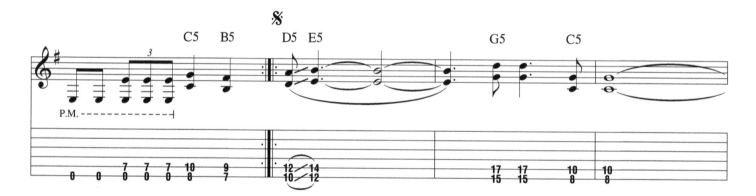

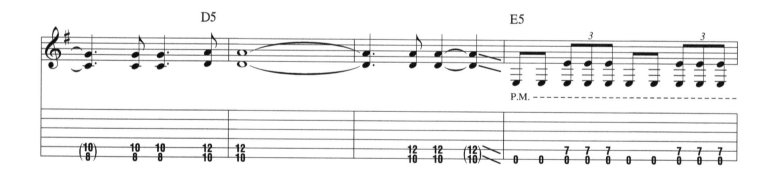

Verse

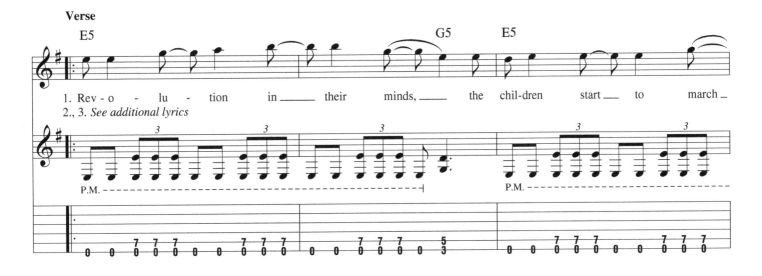

1. Rev - o - lu - tion in _____ their minds, _____ the chil-dren start _____ to march _____
2., 3. *See additional lyrics*

_____ a - gainst the world _____ in which they have to live _____ in. Oh, the

hate that's in _____ their hearts. _____ They're tired of be - ing pushed _____

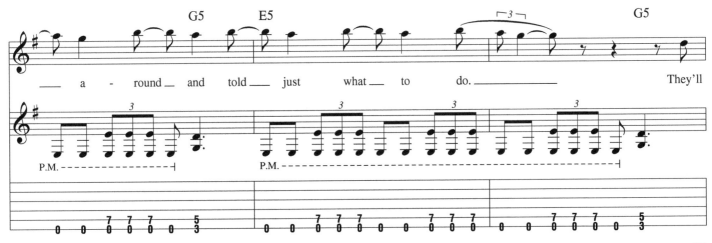

_____ a - round _____ and told _____ just what _____ to do. _____ They'll

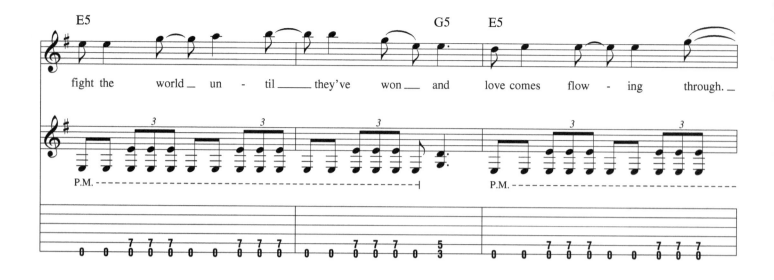

fight the   world ___ un - til ____ they've   won ___ and   love comes   flow - ing   through. __

Interlude

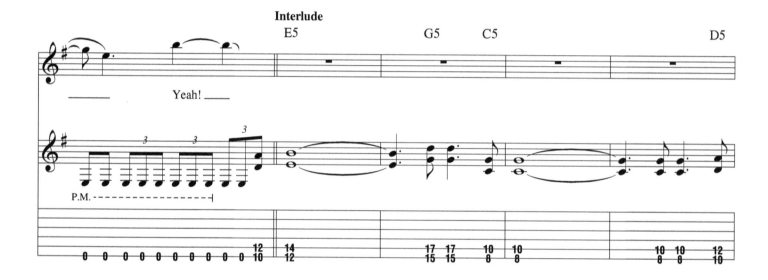

___ ___   Yeah! ___

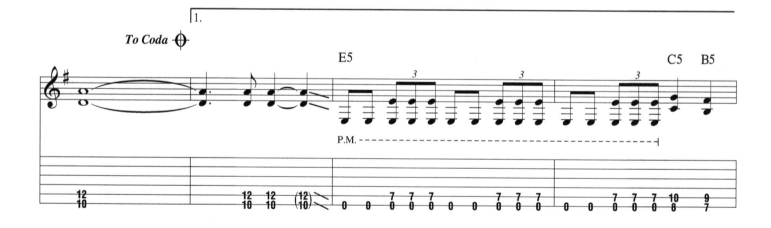

To Coda ⊕

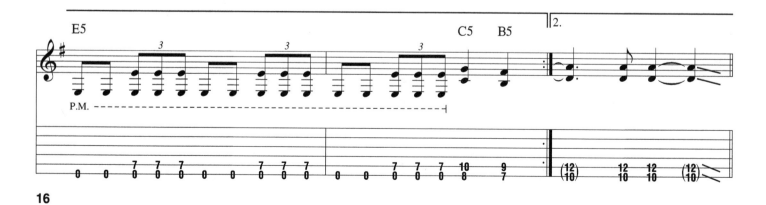

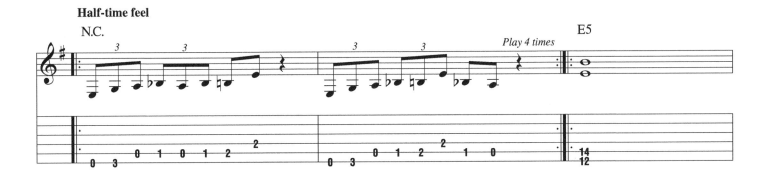

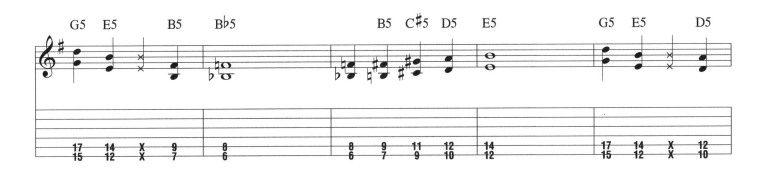

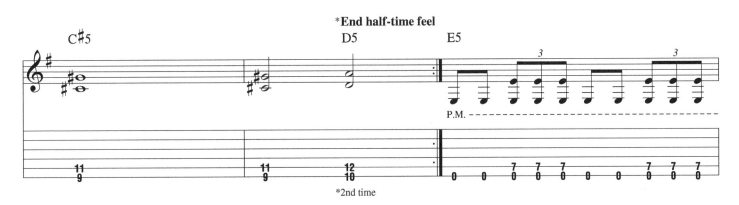

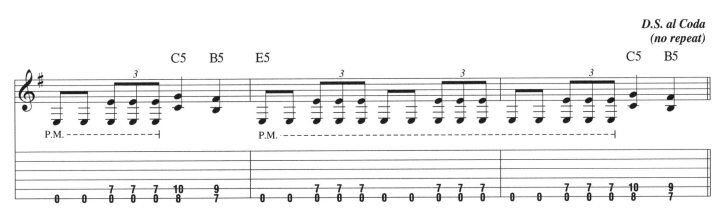

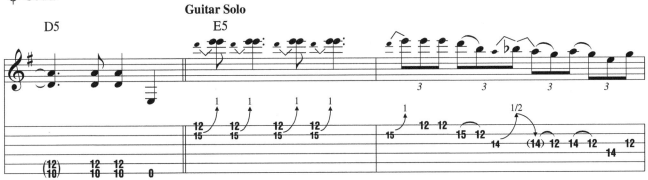

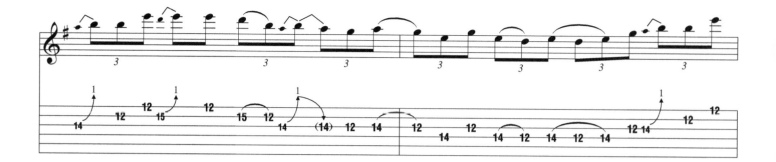

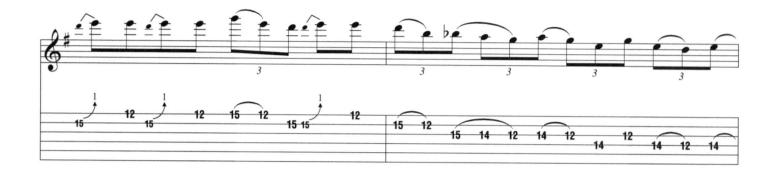

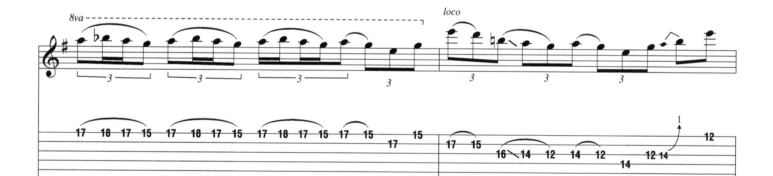

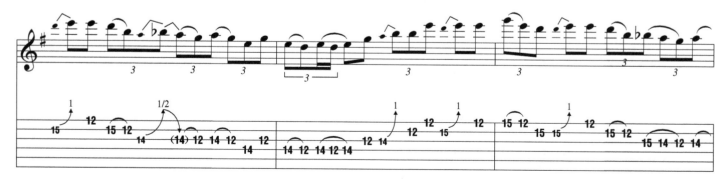

Outro

Additional Lyrics

2. Children of tomorrow live
   In the tears that fall today.
   Will the sunrise of tomorrow
   Bring in peace in any way?
   Must the world live
   In the shadow of atomic fear?
   Can they win the fight for peace
   Or will they disappear? Yeah!

3. So, you children of the world,
   Listen to what I say.
   If you want a better place to live in,
   Spread the words today.
   Show the world that love is still alive.
   You must be brave,
   Or you children of today
   Are children of the grave. Yeah!

N.I.B.

Words and Music by Frank Iommi, Terence Butler, William Ward and John Osbourne

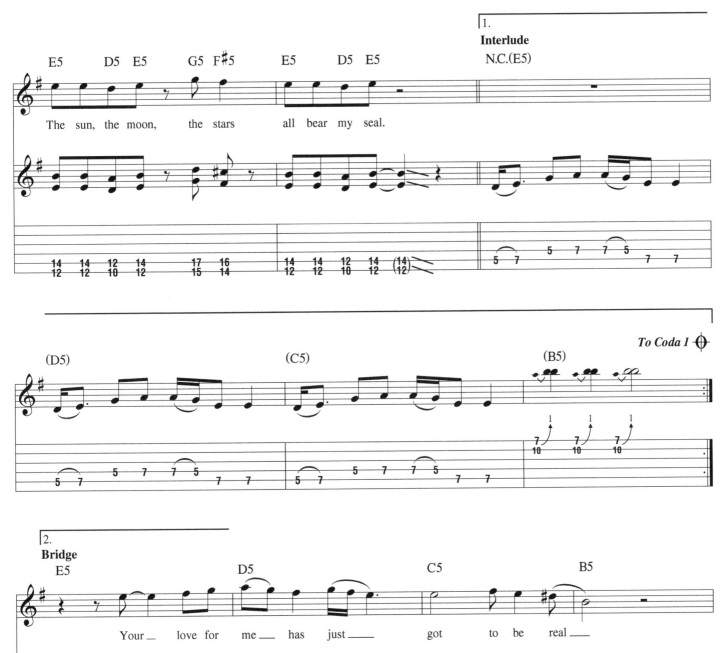

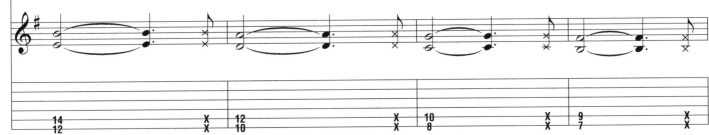

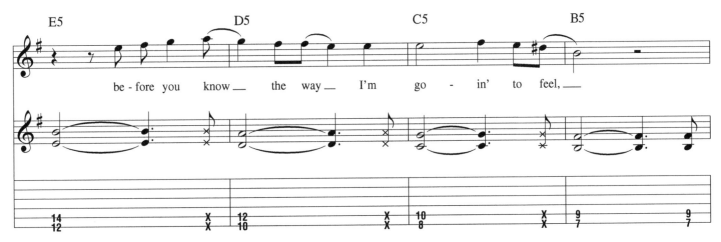

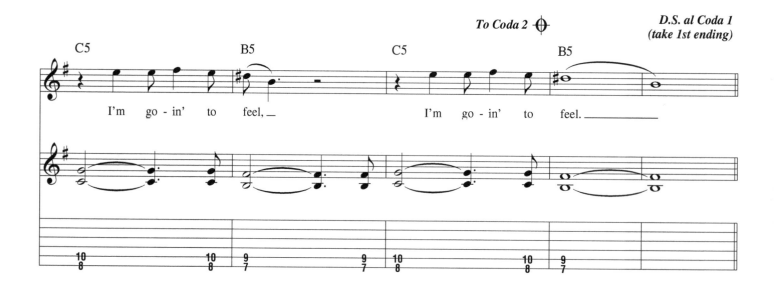

I'm go - in' to feel, ___ I'm go - in' to feel. ___

⊕ **Coda 1**

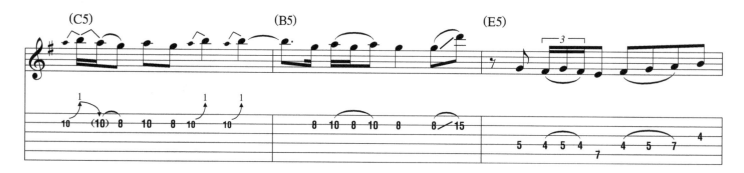

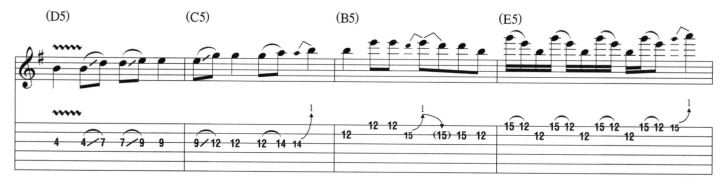

with ev-'ry hour. Look in-to my eyes you'll see who I am.

Outro

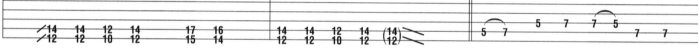

My name is Lu - ci - fer please take my hand.

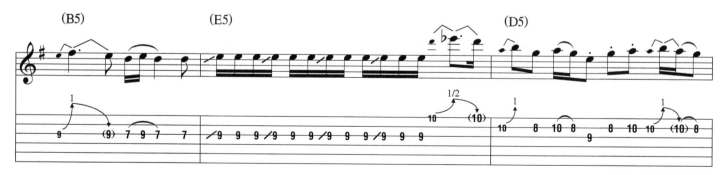

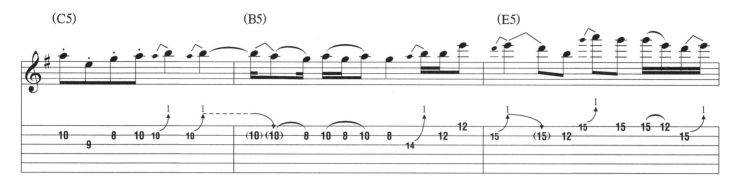

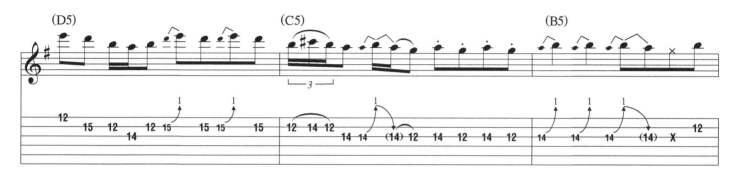

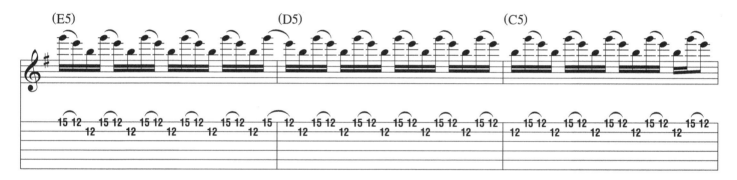

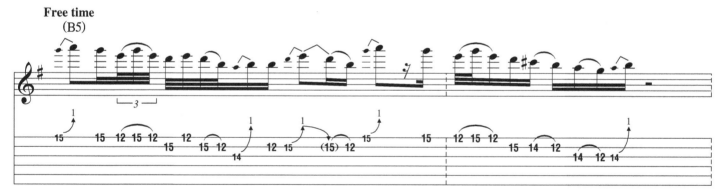

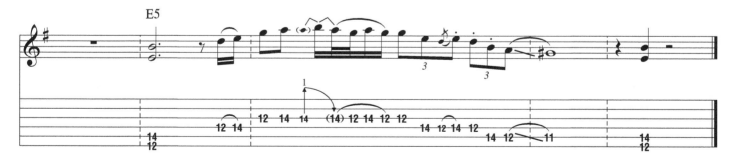

Additional Lyrics

2., 4. Follow me now and you will not regret
　　 Living the life you led before we met.
　　 You are the first to have this love of mine,
　　 Forever with me 'til the end of time.

3. Now I have you with me under my pow'r.
　 Our love grows stronger now with ev'ry hour.
　 Look into my eyes, you'll see who I am.
　 My name is Lucifer, please take my hand.

Paranoid

Words and Music by Anthony Iommi, John Osbourne, William Ward and Terence Butler

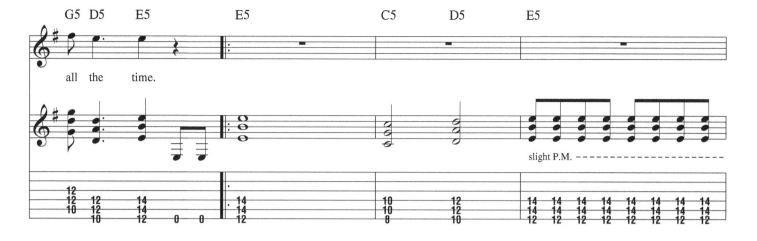

all the time.

Verse

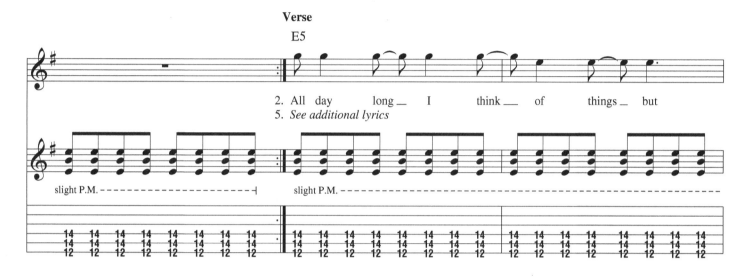

2. All day long __ I think __ of things __ but
5. *See additional lyrics*

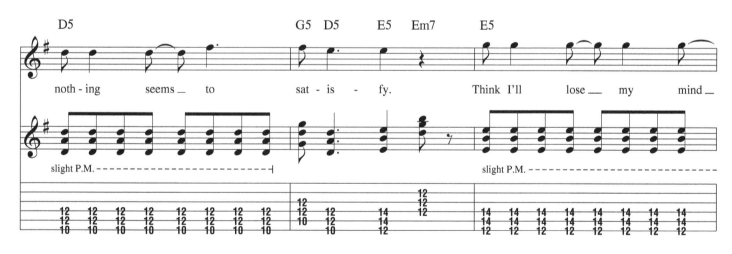

noth - ing seems __ to sat - is - fy. Think I'll lose __ my mind __

To Coda ⊕

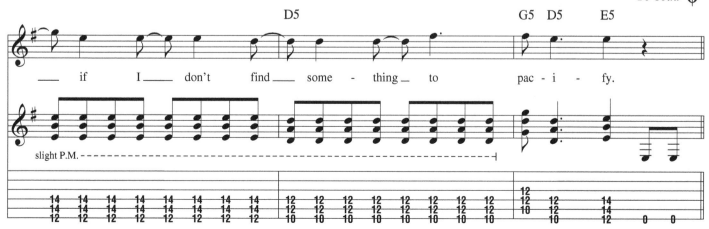

__ if I __ don't find __ some - thing __ to pac - i - fy.

Bridge

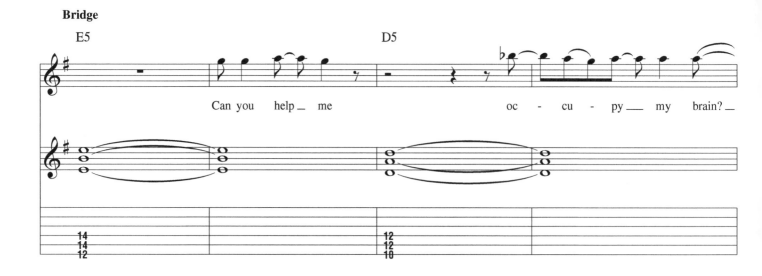

Can you help me oc - cu - py my brain?

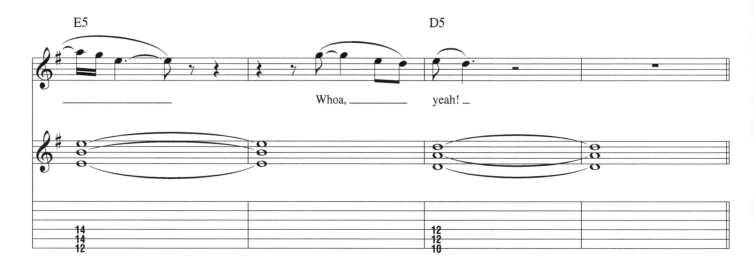

Whoa, yeah!

Interlude

slight P.M.

Verse

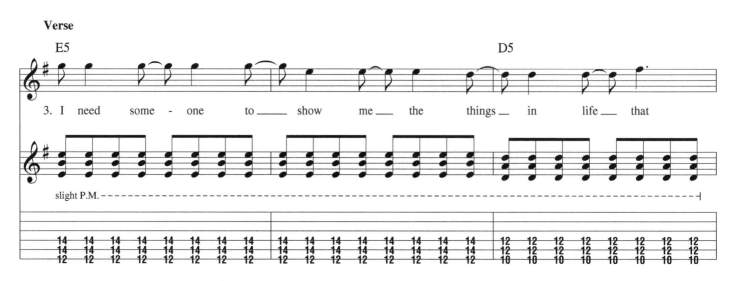

3. I need some - one to show me the things in life that

slight P.M.

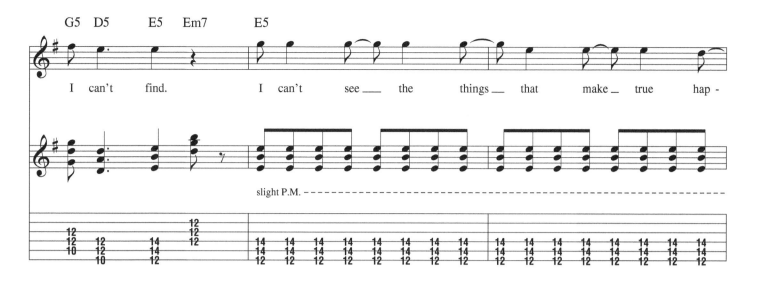

I can't find. I can't see ___ the things ___ that make ___ true hap-

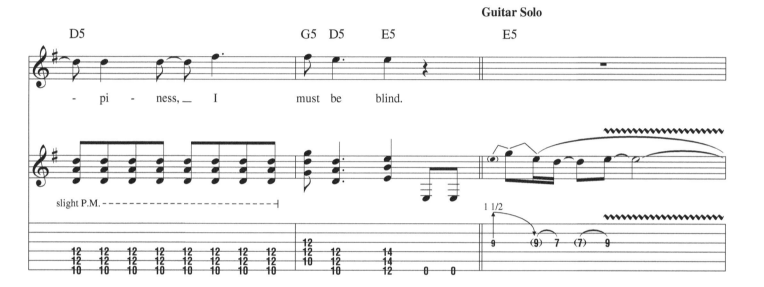

- pi - ness, ___ I must be blind.

Guitar Solo

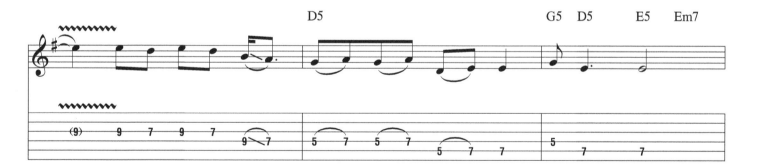

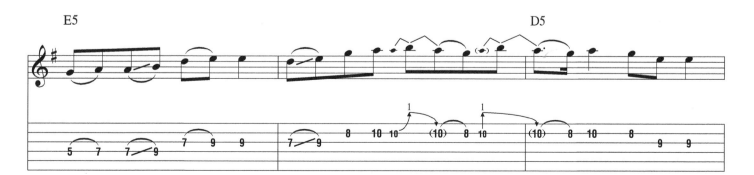

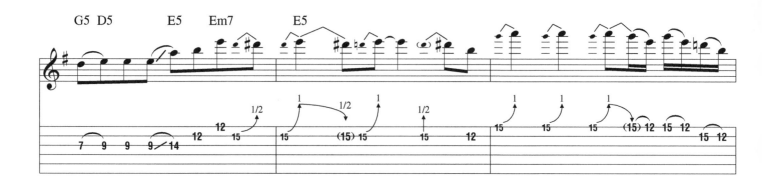

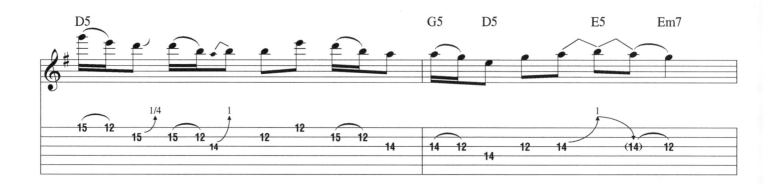

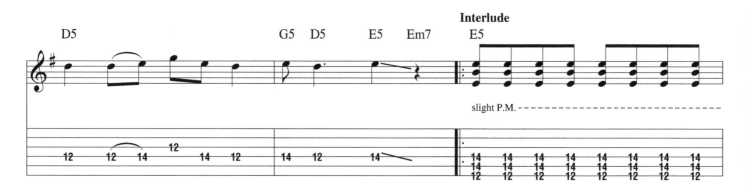

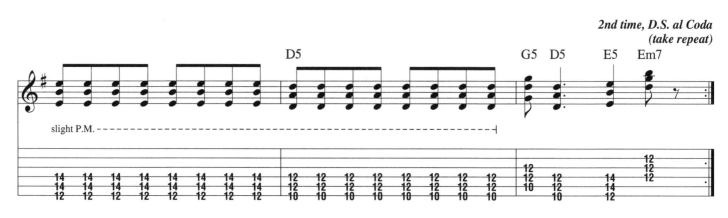

x

Unsupported

2nd time, D.S. al Coda
(take repeat)

x

⊕ Coda

Outro

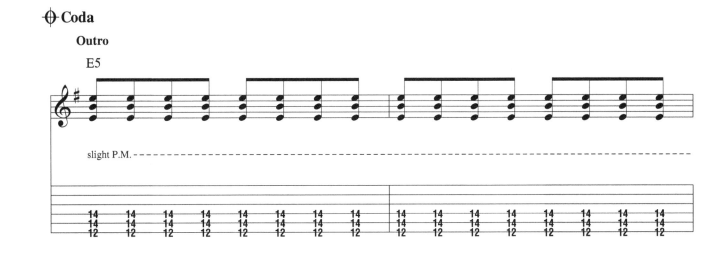

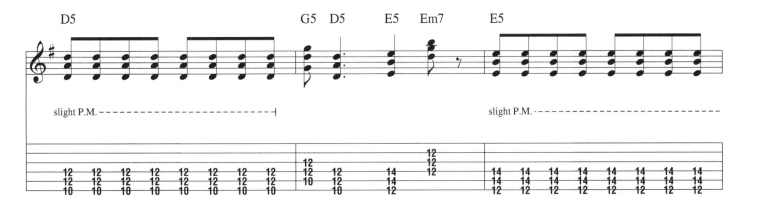

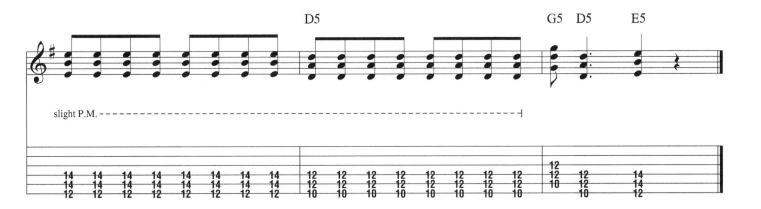

Additional Lyrics

4. Make a joke and I will sigh
   And you will laugh and I will cry.
   Happiness I cannot feel
   And love to me is so unreal.

5. And so as you hear these words
   Telling you now of my state.
   I tell you to enjoy life,
   I wish I could but it's too late.

Sweet Leaf

Words and Music by Frank Iommi, John Osbourne, William Ward and Terence Butler

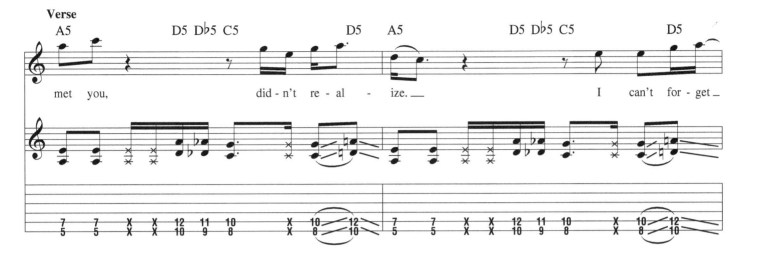

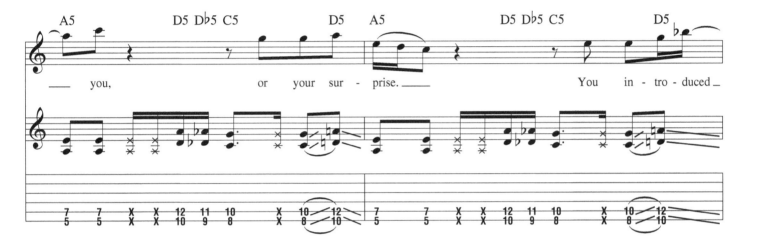

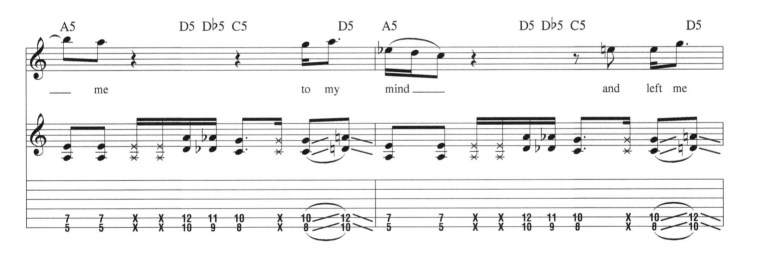

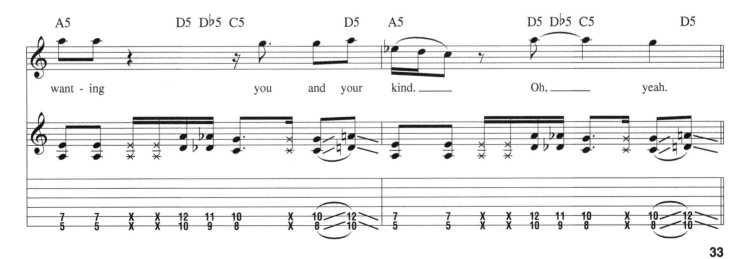

Interlude

Bridge

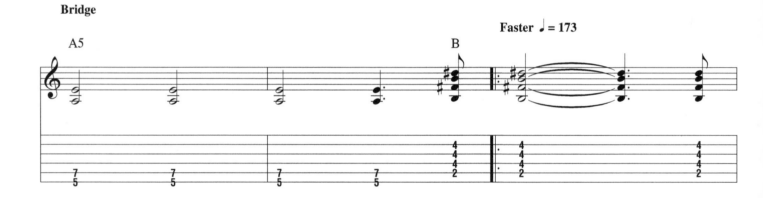

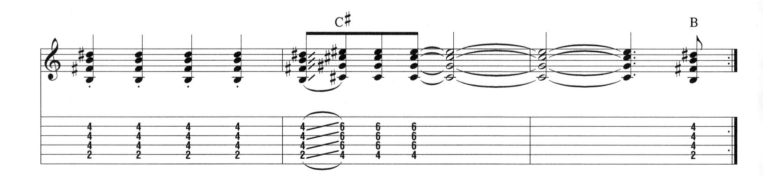

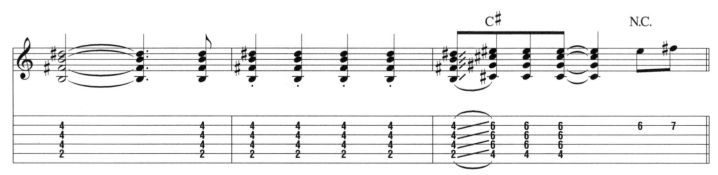

Guitar Solo

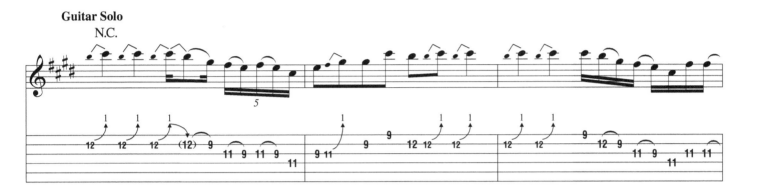

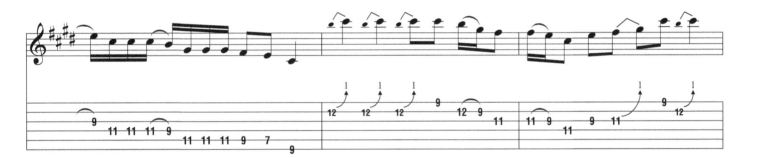

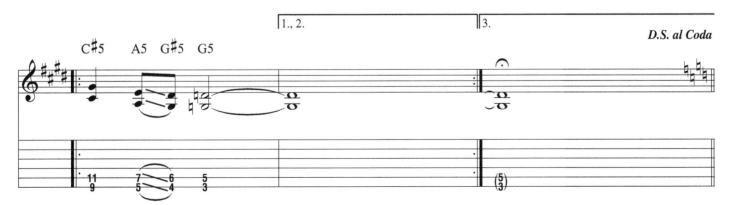

$\bigoplus$ **Coda**

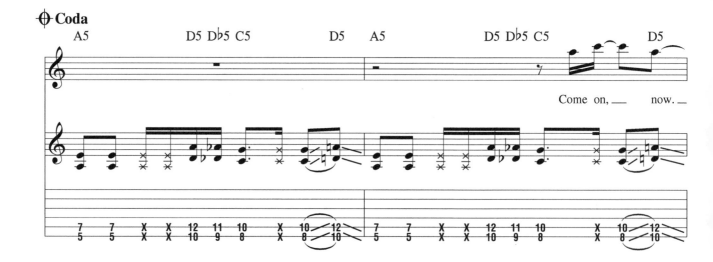

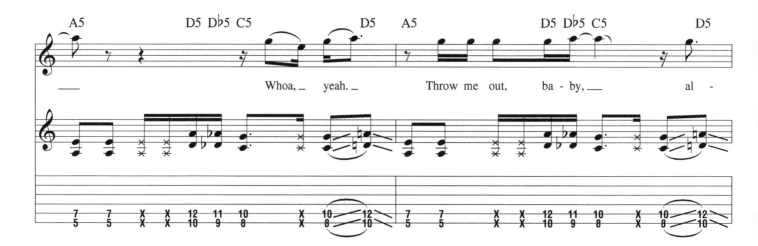

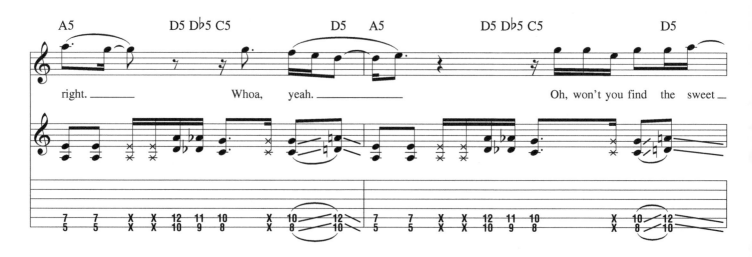

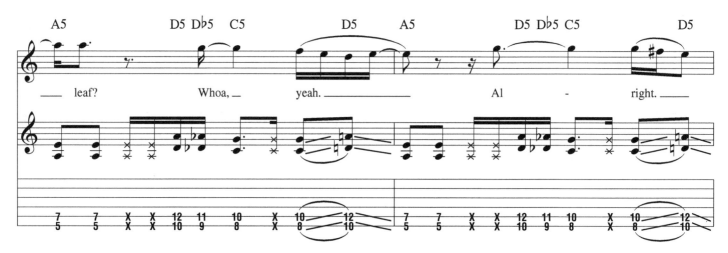

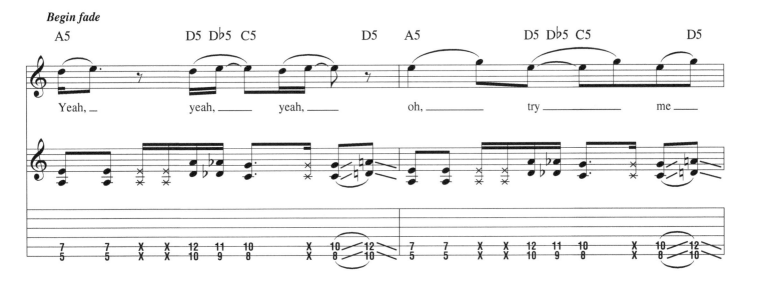

Yeah, __ yeah, _____ yeah, _____ oh, _____ try _____ me __

out. __ I love ya sweet leaf, oh.

Fade out

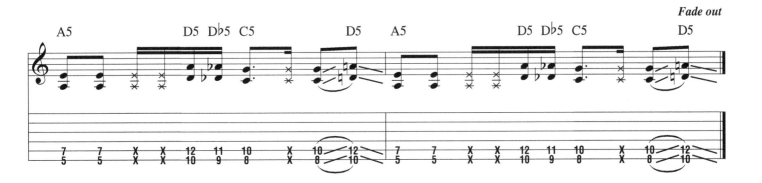

Additional Lyrics

2. My life was empty, forever on a down.
   Until you took me, showed me around.
   My life is free now, my life is clear.
   I love you sweet leaf, though you can't hear.

3. Straight people don't know what you're about.
   They put you down and shut you out.
   You gave to me a new belief.
   And soon the world will love you, sweet leaf.

War Pigs (Interpolating Luke's Wall)

Words and Music by Frank Iommi, John Osbourne, William Ward and Terence Butler

Pre-Intro

Slowly ♩. = 56

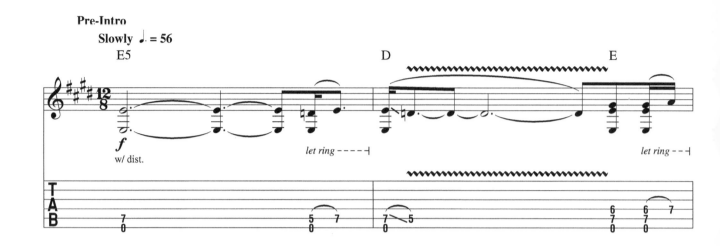

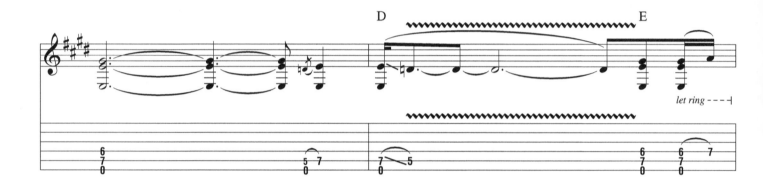

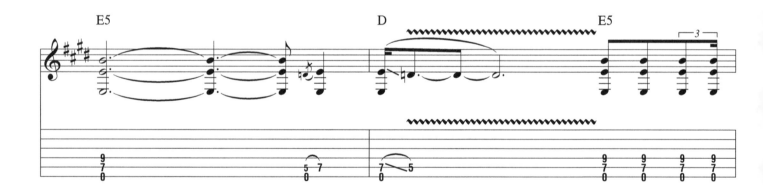

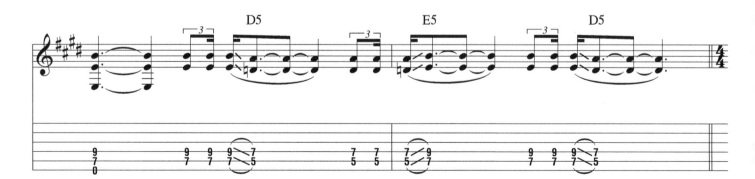

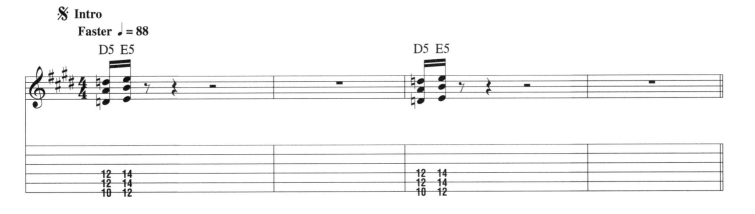

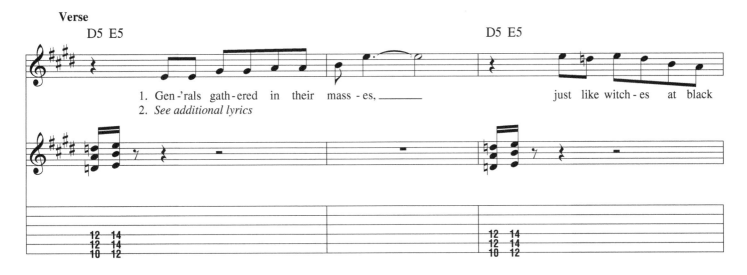

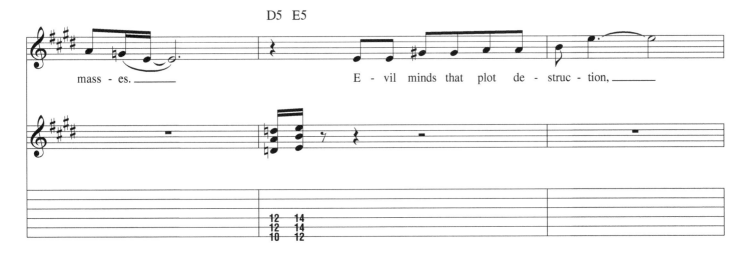

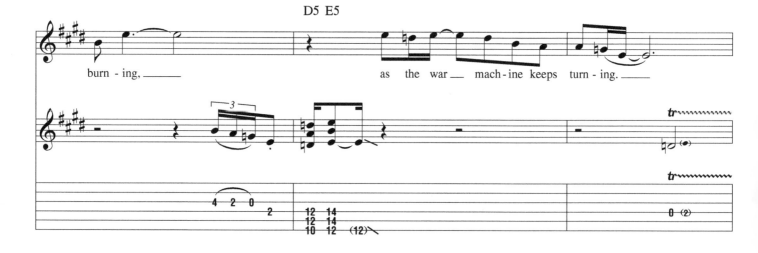

burn - ing, _____ as the war mach-ine keeps turn - ing. _____

Death and ha -tred to man - kind, _____ pois - on - ing _____ their brain-washed

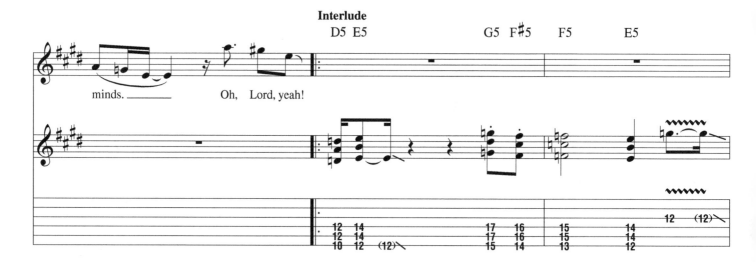

minds. _____ Oh, Lord, yeah!

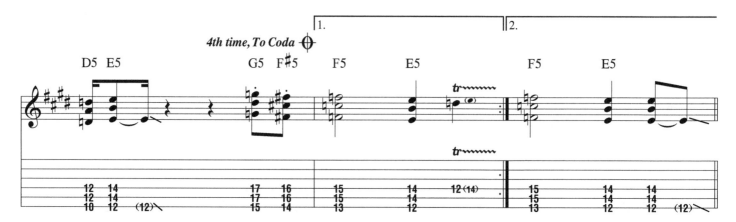

Interlude

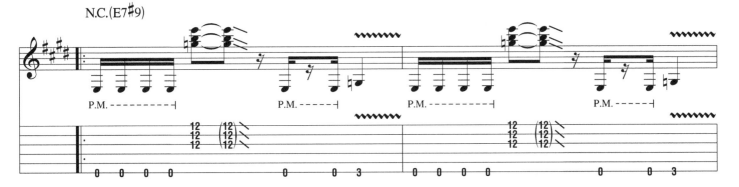

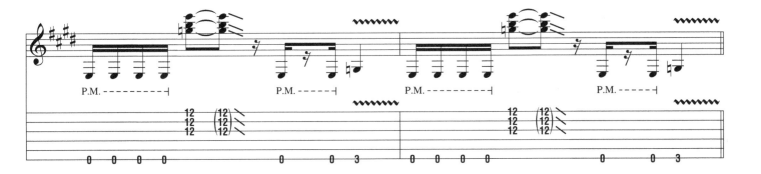

Bridge

Pol - i - ti - cians hide them - selves a - way, ___
See additional lyrics

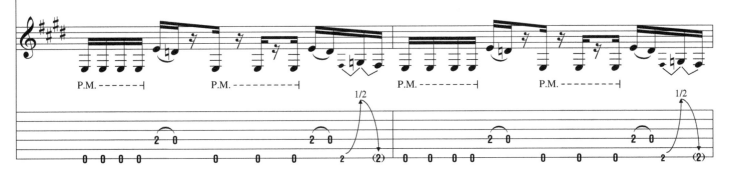

they on - ly start - ed the ___ war. ___

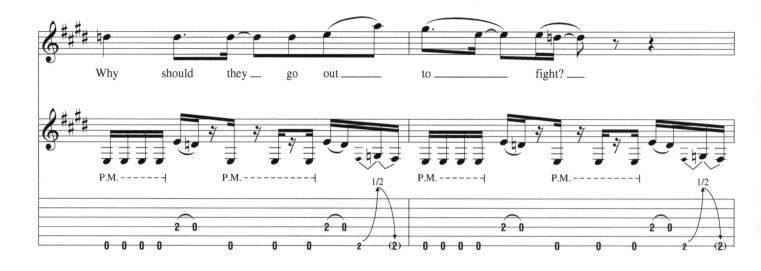

Why should they — go out — to — fight? —

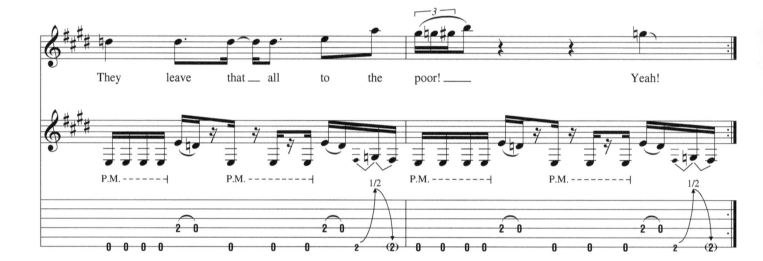

They leave that — all to the poor! — Yeah!

Interlude

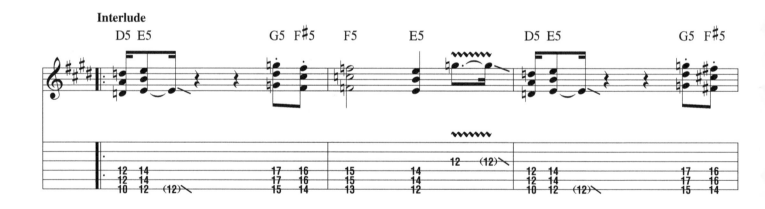

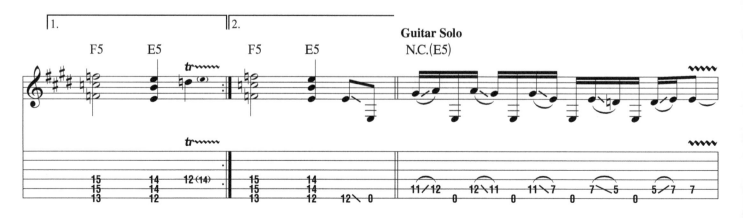

Guitar Solo

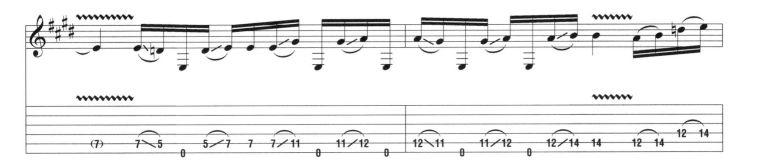

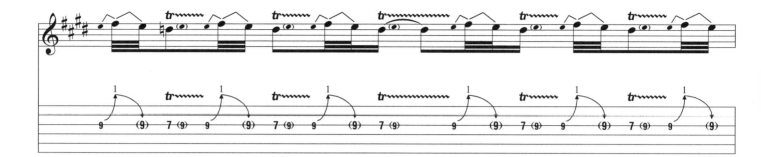

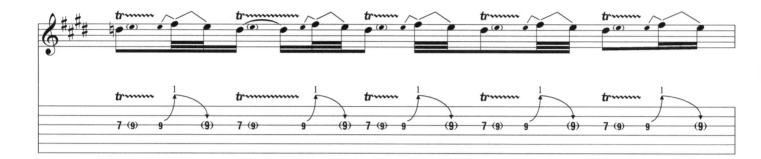

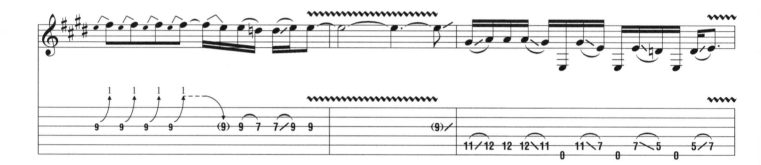

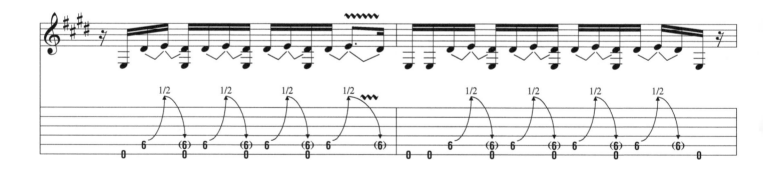

D.S. al Coda
(take repeat)

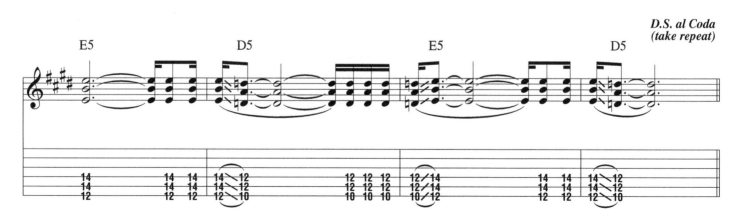

⊕ Coda

A "Luke's Wall"

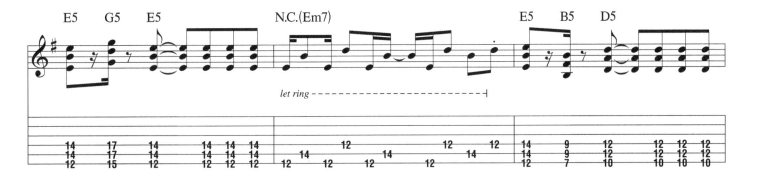

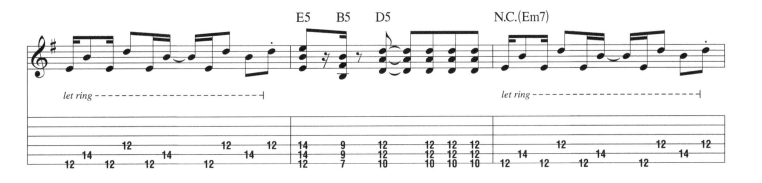

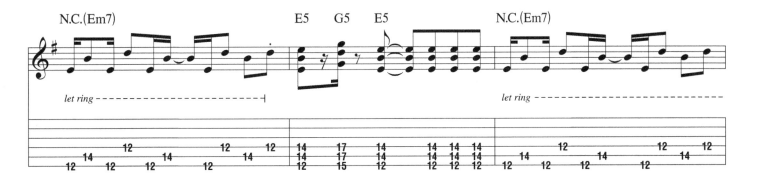

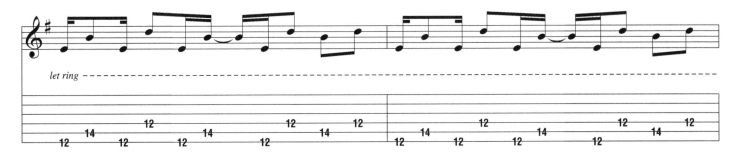

45

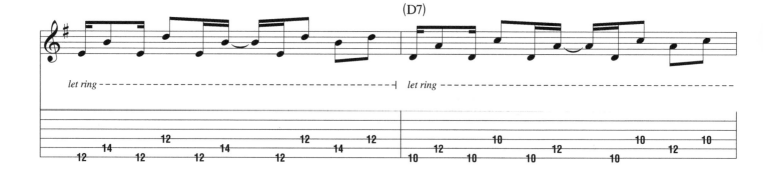

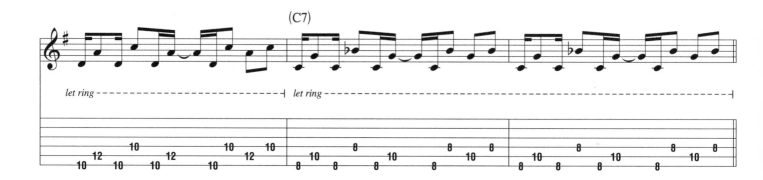

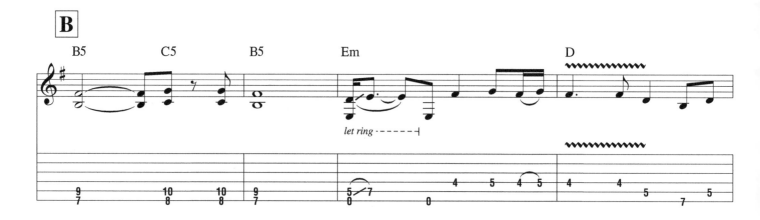

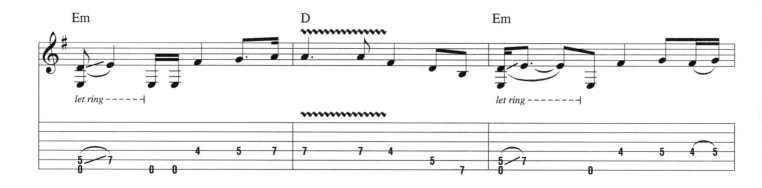

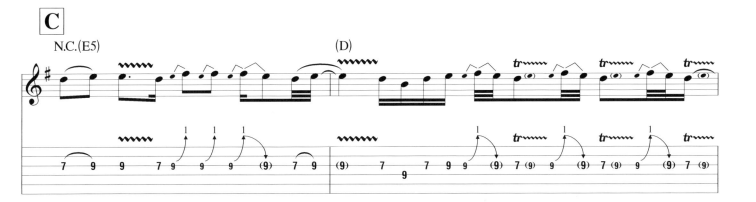

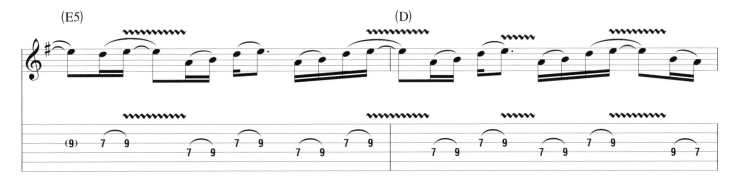

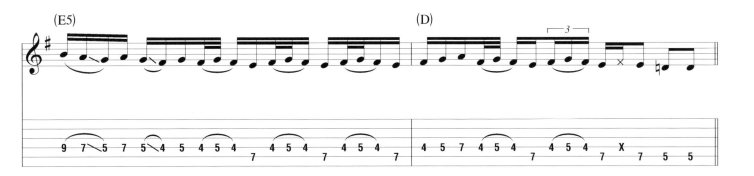

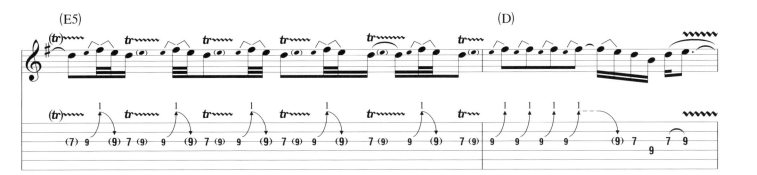

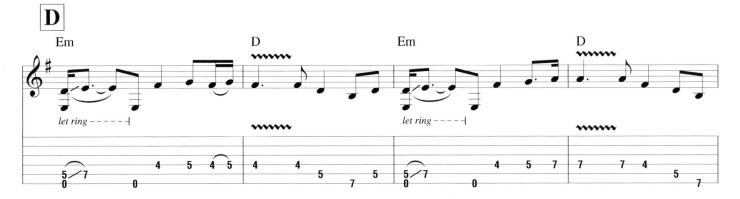

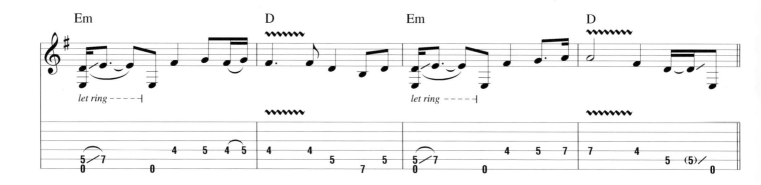

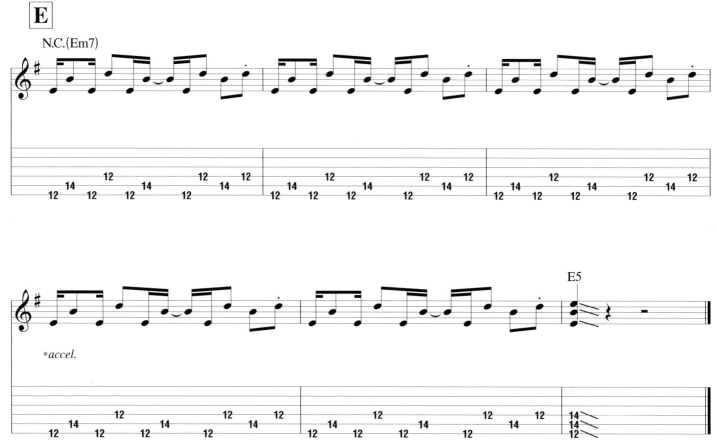

*Tape speeds up; last chord sounds 10 1/2 steps higher.

Additional Lyrics

2. Now in darkness, world stops turning,
Ashes where the bodies burning.
No more war pigs have the power.
Hand of God has struck the hour.
Day of judgment, God is calling,
On their knees, the war pigs crawling.
Begging mercies for their sins,
Satan laughing, spreads his wings.
Oh, Lord, yeah!

Bridge Time will tell on their power minds,
Making war just for fun.
Treating people just like pawns in chess,
Wait till their judgment day comes. Yeah.